3 Times THE Charm

An exciting encore to the original best-seller from Me and My Sister Designs, this book presents 7 more easy little quilts featuring charm squares in 3 color variations. What a great way to get inspired about your fabric collections!

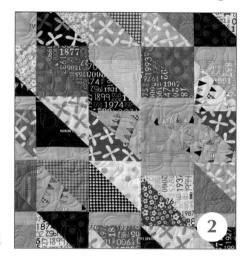
2

6

10

14

18

22

26

LEISURE ARTS, INC. • Little Rock, Arkansas

HANNAH

Finished Quilt Size: 25" x 28" (64 cm x 71 cm)
Finished Block Size: 4" x 4" (10 cm x 10 cm)

SHOPPING LIST

Yardage is based on 43"/44" (109 cm/112 cm) wide fabric.

☐ 1 Charm Pack or 36 assorted 5" x 5" (13 cm x 13 cm) squares
☐ ¼ yd (23 cm) solid color fabric for sashings
☐ 1 yd (91 cm) backing fabric
☐ ⅜ yd (34 cm) binding fabric

You will also need:

☐ 33" x 36" (84 cm x 91 cm) piece of batting

CUTTING THE PIECES

*Follow **Rotary Cutting**, page 30, to cut fabric. Cut all strips from the selvage-to-selvage width of the fabric. Border lengths are exact. All measurements include ¼" seam allowances.*

From fabric for sashings:
• Cut 3 strips 1½" wide. From these strips, cut 18 sashings 1½" x 4½".

From binding fabric:
• Cut 4 **binding strips** 2¼" wide.

MAKING THE BLOCKS

*Follow **Piecing** and **Pressing**, page 32. Match right sides and use ¼" seam allowances throughout. Measurements given include seam allowances.*

1. Divide the 5" x 5" squares into 18 sets of 2 contrasting prints.
2. Draw a diagonal line on the wrong side of the lighter colored square from each set.
3. Place 1 marked **square** on top of the unmarked **square** from the same set. Stitch ¼" from each side of drawn line **(Fig. 1)**. Cut along drawn line and press open to make 2 **Blocks**. Make 36 Blocks. Trim Blocks to 4½" x 4½".

Fig. 1

Block (make 36)

3

ASSEMBLING THE QUILT TOP

1. Referring to **Assembly Diagram** and paying special attention to placement of sashings, sew 6 Blocks and 3 **sashings** together to make *vertical* **Row**. Row should measure 4½" x 27½". Make 6 Rows.
2. Referring to **Quilt Top Diagram**, sew Rows together to make Quilt Top.

COMPLETING THE QUILT

1. Follow **Machine Quilting**, page 33, to mark, layer, and quilt as desired.
2. Follow **Making a Hanging Sleeve**, page 36, to make and attach a hanging sleeve, if desired.
3. Follow **Binding**, page 36, to bind quilt using **binding strips**.

Assembly Diagram

Quilt Top Diagram

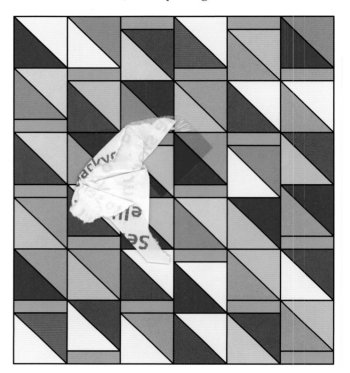

HANNAH

ingrid

Finished Quilt Size: 37½" x 44½" (95 cm x 113 cm)
Finished Block Size: 7" x 7" (18 cm x 18 cm)

SHOPPING LIST

Yardage is based on 43"/44" (109 cm/112 cm) wide fabric.

☐ 1 Charm Pack or 40 assorted 5" x 5" (13 cm x 13 cm) squares
☐ ¾ yd (69 cm) white/light fabric for blocks and inner border
☐ ½ yd (46 cm) of fabric for outer border
☐ 3 yds (2.7 m) backing fabric
☐ ⅜ yd (34 cm) binding fabric

You will also need:

☐ 45" x 52" (114 cm x 132 cm) piece of batting

CUTTING THE PIECES

*Follow **Rotary Cutting**, page 30, to cut fabric. Cut all strips from the selvage-to-selvage width of the fabric. Border lengths are exact. All measurements include ¼" seam allowances.*

From Charm Pack or assorted squares:
• From *each* of 20 squares, cut 2 **large rectangles** 2½" x 5" (**Cutting Diagram A**).
• From *each* of remaining 20 squares, cut 3 **small rectangles** 1½" x 5" (**Cutting Diagram B**).

From white/light fabric:
• Cut 8 strips 1¾" wide. From these strips, cut 40 **long rectangles** 1¾" x 7½".
• Cut 2 **side inner borders** 1¾" x 35½".
• Cut 2 **top/bottom inner borders** 1¾" x 31".

From fabric for outer border:
• Cut 2 **side outer borders** 3½" x 38".
• Cut 2 **top/bottom outer borders** 3½" x 37".

From binding fabric:
• Cut 5 **binding strips** 2¼" wide.

Cutting Diagram A

2½" x 5"	2½" x 5"

Cutting Diagram B

1½" x 5"	1½" x 5"	1½" x 5"	

MAKING THE BLOCKS

*Follow **Piecing and Pressing**, page 32. Match right sides and use ¹/₄" seam allowances throughout. Measurements given include seam allowances.*

1. Sew 3 assorted **small rectangles** together to make **Unit 1**. Make 20 Unit 1's.

Unit 1 (make 20)

2. Sew 2 matching **large rectangles** and 1 Unit 1 together to make **Unit 2**. Make 20 Unit 2's.

Unit 2 (make 20)

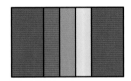

3. Sew 2 **long rectangles** and 1 Unit 2 together to make **Block**. Block should measure 7¹/₂" x 7¹/₂". Make 20 Blocks.

Block (make 20)

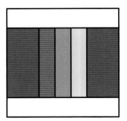

ASSEMBLING THE QUILT TOP

1. Rotating Blocks as shown, sew 4 Blocks together to make **Row**. Row should measure 28¹/₂" x 7¹/₂". Make 5 Rows.

Row (make 5)

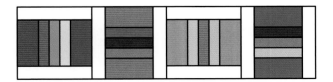

2. Referring to **Quilt Top Diagram** and rotating every other Row, sew Rows together to make **Quilt Top Center**. Quilt Top Center should measure 28¹/₂" x 35¹/₂".
3. Matching centers and corners, sew **side** and then **top/bottom inner borders** to Quilt Top Center.
4. Matching centers and corners, sew **side** and then **top/bottom outer borders** to Quilt Top.

COMPLETING THE QUILT

1. Follow **Machine Quilting**, page 33, to mark, layer, and quilt as desired.
2. Follow **Making a Hanging Sleeve**, page 36, to make and attach a hanging sleeve, if desired.
3. Follow **Binding**, page 36, to bind quilt using **binding strips**.

Quilt Top Diagram

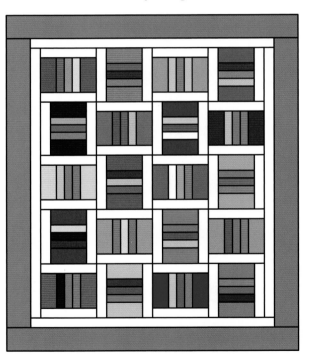

ingrid

jennifer

Finished Quilt Size: 39" x 47" (99 cm x 119 cm)
Finished Block Size: 4" x 8" (10 cm x 20 cm)

SHOPPING LIST

Yardage is based on 43"/44" (109 cm/112 cm) wide fabric.

- ☐ 1 Charm Pack or 40 assorted 5" x 5" (13 cm x 13 cm) squares
- ☐ 1¼ yds (1.1 m) white/light fabric for blocks and border
- ☐ 3⅛ yds (2.9 m) backing fabric
- ☐ ⅜ yd (34 cm) binding fabric

You will also need:

- ☐ 47" x 55" (119 cm x 140 cm) piece of batting

CUTTING THE PIECES

*Follow **Rotary Cutting**, page 30, to cut fabric. Cut all strips from the selvage-to-selvage width of the fabric. Border lengths are exact. All measurements include ¼" seam allowances.*

From white/light fabric:
- Cut 5 strips 5" wide. From these strips, cut 40 **squares** 5" x 5".
- Cut 2 **side borders** 3½" x 40½", pieced as needed.
- Cut 2 **top/bottom borders** 3½" x 38½".

From binding fabric:
- Cut 5 **binding strips** 2¼" wide.

MAKING THE BLOCKS

*Follow **Piecing** and **Pressing**, page 32. Match right sides and use ¼" seam allowances throughout. Measurements given include seam allowances.*

1. Draw a diagonal line on the wrong side of each white/light **square**.
2. Place 1 white/light **square** on top of 1 charm **square**. Stitch ¼" from each side of drawn line (**Fig. 1**). Cut along drawn line and press open to make 2 **Triangle-Squares**. Make 80 Triangle-Squares. Trim Triangle-Squares to 4½" x 4½".

Fig. 1   Triangle-Square (make 80)

3. Sew 2 Triangles-Squares together to make **Block**. Block should measure 4½" x 8½". Make 20 **Block A's** and 20 **Block B's**.

Block A   Block B
(make 20)   (make 20)

   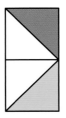

ASSEMBLING THE QUILT TOP

1. Referring to **Assembly Diagram**, sew 5 Block A's together to make *vertical* **Row A**. Row A should measure $4^1/2$" x $40^1/2$". Make 4 Row A's.

2. Sew 5 Block B's together to make *vertical* **Row B**. Row B should measure $4^1/2$" x $40^1/2$". Make 4 Row B's.

3. Rotating Rows as shown, sew Rows together to make **Quilt Top Center**. Quilt Top Center should measure $32^1/2$" x $40^1/2$".

4. Referring to **Quilt Top Diagram** and matching centers and corners, sew **side** and then **top/bottom borders** to Quilt Top Center.

COMPLETING THE QUILT

1. Follow **Machine Quilting**, page 33, to mark, layer, and quilt as desired.

2. Follow **Making a Hanging Sleeve**, page 36, to make and attach a hanging sleeve, if desired.

3. Follow **Binding**, page 36, to bind quilt using **binding strips**.

Quilt Top Diagram

Assembly Diagram

A   B   B   A   A   B   B   A

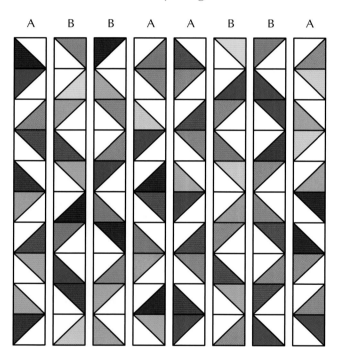

JENNiFER

KENDRA

Finished Quilt Size: 37½" x 37½" (95 cm x 95 cm)
Finished Block Size: 4½" x 4½" (11 cm x 11 cm)

SHOPPING LIST

Yardage is based on 43"/44" (109 cm/112 cm) wide fabric.

☐ 1 Charm Pack or 34 assorted 5" x 5" (13 cm x 13 cm) squares

☐ 1 yd (91 cm) white/light fabric for blocks, sashings, and inner borders

☐ ⅝ yd (57 cm) fabric for outer border

☐ 2½ yds (2.3 m) backing fabric

☐ ⅜ yd (34 cm) binding fabric

You will also need:

☐ 45" x 45" (114 cm x 114 cm) piece of batting

CUTTING THE PIECES

*Follow **Rotary Cutting**, page 30, to cut fabric. Cut all strips from the selvage-to-selvage width of the fabric. Border lengths are exact. All measurements include ¼" seam allowances.*

From Charm Pack or assorted squares:

- From *each* of 25 squares, cut 2 **large rectangles** 2¼" x 5" **(Cutting Diagram A)**.
- From *each* of remaining 9 squares, cut 3 **small rectangles** 1½" x 5" **(Cutting Diagram B)**. You will use 25 and have 2 left over.

From white/light fabric:

- Cut 6 strips 2¼" wide. From these strips, cut 100 **squares** 2¼" x 2¼".
- Cut 3 strips 1½" wide. From these strips, cut 20 **vertical sashings** 1½" x 5".
- Cut 4 **horizontal sashings** 1½" x 27".
- Cut 2 **side inner borders** 1½" x 27".
- Cut 2 **top/bottom inner borders** 1½" x 29".

From fabric for outer border:

- Cut 2 **side outer borders** 4½" x 29".
- Cut 2 **top/bottom outer borders** 4½" x 37".

From binding fabric:

- Cut 5 **binding strips** 2¼" wide.

Cutting Diagram A

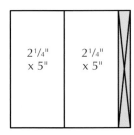

2¼" x 5" 2¼" x 5"

Cutting Diagram B

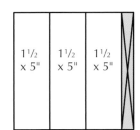

1½ x 5" 1½ x 5" 1½ x 5"

MAKING THE BLOCKS

*Follow **Piecing** and **Pressing**, page 32. Match right sides and use ¹/₄" seam allowances throughout. Measurements given include seam allowances.*

1. Draw a diagonal line on the wrong side of each **square**.
2. Place 2 **squares** on the short sides of 1 **large rectangle** and stitch along drawn lines **(Fig. 1)**. Trim ¹/₄" from stitching lines **(Fig. 2)** and press open to make **Unit 1**. Make 50 (25 pairs of matching) Unit 1's.

Fig. 1	**Fig. 2**
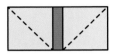	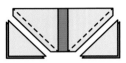

Unit 1 (make 50)

3. Sew 1 **small rectangle** and 2 matching Unit 1's together to make **Block**. Block should measure 5" x 5". Make 25 Blocks.

Block (make 25)

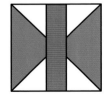

ASSEMBLING THE QUILT TOP

1. Rotating Blocks as shown, sew 5 Blocks and 4 **vertical sashings** together to make **Row A**. Row A should measure 27" x 5". Make 3 Row A's.

Row A (make 3)

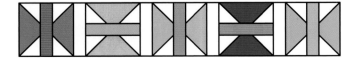

2. Rotating Blocks as shown, sew 5 Blocks and 4 vertical sashings together to make **Row B**. Row B should measure 27" x 5". Make 2 Row B's.

Row B (make 2)

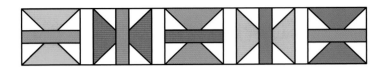

3. Referring to **Quilt Top Diagram**, sew Rows and 4 **horizontal sashings** together to make **Quilt Top Center**. Quilt Top Center should measure 27" x 27".
4. Matching centers and corners, sew **side** and then **top/bottom inner borders** to Quilt Top Center.
5. Matching centers and corners, sew **side** and then **top/bottom outer borders** to Quilt Top.

COMPLETING THE QUILT

1. Follow **Machine Quilting**, page 33, to mark, layer, and quilt as desired.
2. Follow **Making a Hanging Sleeve**, page 36, to make and attach a hanging sleeve, if desired.
3. Follow **Binding**, page 36, to bind quilt using **binding strips**.

Quilt Top Diagram

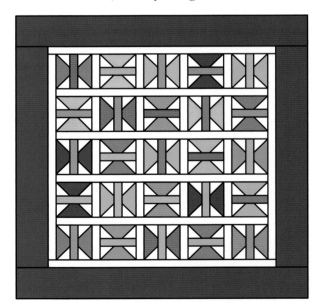

kendra

LESLIE

Finished Quilt Size: 33" x 33" (84 cm x 84 cm)
Finished Block Size: 4" x 4" (10 cm x 10 cm)

SHOPPING LIST

Yardage is based on 43"/44" (109 cm/112 cm) wide fabric.

☐ 1 Charm Pack or 36 assorted 5" x 5" (13 cm x 13 cm) squares
☐ ³⁄₈ yd (34 cm) solid white or color fabric for blocks and inner border
☐ ¹⁄₂ yd (46 cm) fabric for outer border
☐ 1¹⁄₄ yds (1.1 m) backing fabric
☐ ³⁄₈ yd (34 cm) binding fabric

You will also need:

☐ 41" x 41 (104 cm x 104" cm) piece of batting

CUTTING THE PIECES

*Follow **Rotary Cutting**, page 30, to cut fabric. Cut all strips from the selvage-to-selvage width of the fabric. Border lengths are exact. All measurements include ¹⁄₄" seam allowances.*

From *each* charm square or assorted square:
- Cut 1 **medium rectangle** 2" x 4¹⁄₂" and 1 **large rectangle** 3" x 4¹⁄₂" (**Cutting Diagram**).

From solid white or color fabric:
- Cut 5 strips 1" wide. From these strips, cut 36 **small rectangles** 1" x 4¹⁄₂".
- Cut 2 **side inner borders** 1¹⁄₂" x 24¹⁄₂".
- Cut 2 **top/bottom inner borders** 1¹⁄₂" x 26¹⁄₂".

From fabric for outer border:
- Cut 2 **side outer borders** 3¹⁄₂" x 26¹⁄₂".
- Cut 2 **top/bottom outer borders** 3¹⁄₂" x 32¹⁄₂".

From binding fabric:
- Cut 4 **binding strips** 2¹⁄₄" wide.

Cutting Diagram

2" x 4¹⁄₂"	3" x 4¹⁄₂"

MAKING THE BLOCKS

Follow Piecing and Pressing, page 32. Match right sides and use ¹/₄" seam allowances throughout. Measurements given include seam allowances.

1. Sew 1 **medium rectangle** and 1 **large rectangle** together to make **Unit 1**. Make 36 Unit 1's.

Unit 1 (make 36)

2. Cut 1 Unit 1 in half (**Fig. 1**) to make 2 **Unit 2's**. Make 72 Unit 2's.

Fig. 1   **Unit 2** (make 72)

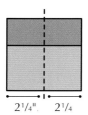   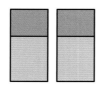

2¹/₄"   2¹/₄

3. Sew 2 matching Unit 2's and 1 **small rectangle** together to make **Block**. Block should measure 4¹/₂" x 4¹/₂". Make 36 Blocks.

Block (make 36)

ASSEMBLING THE QUILT TOP

1. Rotating Blocks as shown, sew 6 Blocks together to make **Row**. Row should measure 24¹/₂" x 4¹/₂". Make 6 Rows.

Row (make 6)

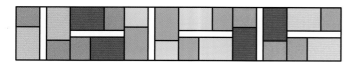

2. Referring to **Quilt Top Diagram** and rotating every other Row, sew Rows together to make **Quilt Top Center**. Quilt Top Center should measure 24¹/₂" x 24¹/₂".

3. Matching centers and corners, sew **side** and then **top/bottom inner borders** to Quilt Top Center.

4. Matching centers and corners, sew **side** and then **top/bottom outer borders** to Quilt Top.

COMPLETING THE QUILT

1. Follow **Machine Quilting**, page 33, to mark, layer, and quilt as desired.

2. Follow **Making a Hanging Sleeve**, page 36, to make and attach a hanging sleeve, if desired.

3. Follow **Binding**, page 36, to bind quilt using **binding strips**.

Quilt Top Diagram

LESLIE

For these versions, you will need ¼ yd (23 cm) of fabric for the small rectangles and ¼ yd (23 cm) of fabric for the inner borders.

MOLLY

Finished Quilt Size: 40½" x 40½" (103 cm x 103 cm)
Finished Block Size: 8½" x 8½" (22 cm x 22 cm)

SHOPPING LIST

Yardage is based on 43"/44" (109 cm/112 cm) wide fabric.

☐ 1 Charm Pack or 36 assorted 5" x 5" (13 cm x 13 cm) squares

☐ ⅝ yd (57 cm) white/light fabric for sashings and inner borders

☐ ⅛ yd (11 cm) **each** of 4 fabrics for outer border

☐ 2¾ yds (2.5 m) backing fabric

☐ ⅜ yd (34 cm) binding fabric

You will also need:

☐ 48" x 48" (122 cm x 122 cm) piece of batting

CUTTING THE PIECES

*Follow **Rotary Cutting**, page 30, to cut fabric. Cut all strips from the selvage-to-selvage width of the fabric. Border lengths are exact. All measurements include ¼" seam allowances.*

From Charm Pack or assorted squares:
• Set aside 9 squares for **block centers**.
• From **each** of remaining 27 squares, cut 2 **large rectangles** 2½" x 5" (**Cutting Diagram A**). Set aside 18 assorted large rectangles.
• Trim remaining 36 large rectangles to make 36 **small rectangles** 2½" x 4¾" (**Cutting Diagram B**).

From white/light fabric:
• Cut 2 strips 2½" wide. From these strips, cut 6 **vertical sashings** 2½" x 9".
• Cut 2 **horizontal sashings** 2½" x 30".
• Cut 2 **side inner borders** 2½" x 30".
• Cut 2 **top/bottom inner borders** 2½" x 34".

From fabrics for outer border:
• Cut 2 **side outer borders** 3½" x 34".
• Cut 2 **top/bottom outer borders** 3½" x 40".

From binding fabric:
• Cut 5 **binding strips** 2¼" wide.

Cutting Diagram A

2½" x 5"	2½" x 5"

Cutting Diagram B

2½" x 4¾"

MAKING THE BLOCKS

Follow Piecing and Pressing, page 32. Match right sides and use ¹/₄" seam allowances throughout. Measurements given include seam allowances.

1. Sew 2 **small rectangles** together to make **Unit 1**. Make 18 Unit 1's.

Unit 1 (make 18)

2. Sew 2 **large rectangles** and 1 **block center** together to make **Unit 2**. Make 9 Unit 2's.

Unit 2 (make 9)

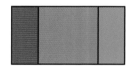

3. Sew 2 Unit 1's and 1 Unit 2 together to make **Block**. Block should measure 9" x 9". Make 9 Blocks.

Block (make 9)

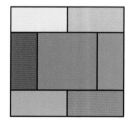

ASSEMBLING THE QUILT TOP

1. Rotating Blocks as shown, sew 3 Blocks and 2 **vertical sashings** together to make **Row A**. Row A should measure 30" x 9". Make 2 Row A's.

Row A (make 2)

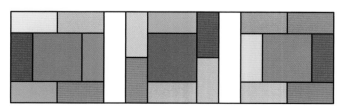

2. Rotating Blocks as shown, sew 3 Blocks and 2 vertical sashings together to make **Row B**. Row B should measure 30" x 9".

Row B

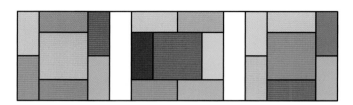

3. Referring to **Quilt Top Diagram**, sew Rows and 2 **horizontal sashings** together to make **Quilt Top Center**. Quilt Top Center should measure 30" x 30".
4. Matching centers and corners, sew **side** and then **top/bottom inner borders** to Quilt Top Center.
5. Matching centers and corners, sew **side** and then **top/bottom outer borders** to Quilt Top.

COMPLETING THE QUILT

1. Follow **Machine Quilting**, page 33, to mark, layer, and quilt as desired.
2. Follow **Making a Hanging Sleeve**, page 36, to make and attach a hanging sleeve, if desired.
3. Follow **Binding**, page 36, to bind quilt using **binding strips**.

Quilt Top Diagram

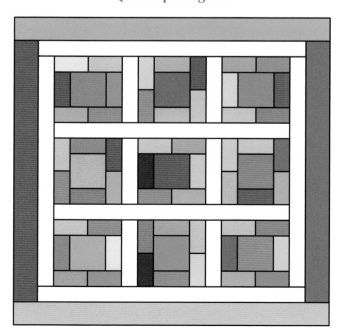

MOLLY

NiCOLE

Finished Quilt Size: 36³/₄" x 42¹/₂" (93 cm x 108 cm)
Finished Block Size: 4³/₄" x 6¹/₂" (12 cm x 17 cm)

SHOPPING LIST

Yardage is based on 43"/44" (109 cm/112 cm) wide fabric.

☐ 1 Charm Pack or 25 assorted 5" x 5" (13 cm x 13 cm) squares
☐ 1 yd (91 cm) white/light fabric for blocks, sashings, and inner border
☐ ¹/₂ yd (46 cm) of fabric for block bottoms and outer border
☐ ¹/₄ yd (23 cm) of fabric for middle border
☐ 2⁷/₈ yds (2.6 m) backing fabric
☐ ³/₈ yd (34 cm) binding fabric

You will also need:

☐ 44" x 50" (112 cm x 127 cm) piece of batting

CUTTING THE PIECES

*Follow **Rotary Cutting**, page 30, to cut fabric. Cut all strips from the selvage-to-selvage width of the fabric. Border lengths are exact. All measurements include ¹/₄" seam allowances.*

From each charm square or assorted square:
• Cut 1 **rectangle A** 3¹/₂" x 3", **1 rectangle B** 2¹/₄" x 2", and 5 **squares** 1¹/₄" x 1¹/₄" (**Cutting Diagram**).

From white/light fabric:
• Cut 3 strips 2³/₄" wide. From these strips, cut 25 **rectangles C** 3¹/₂" x 2³/₄".
• Cut 3 strips 2¹/₄" wide. From these strips, cut 25 **rectangles D** 2¹/₄" x 3³/₄".
• Cut 3 strips 1¹/₄" wide. From these strips, cut 25 **rectangles E** 2¹/₄" x 1¹/₄" and 25 **rectangles F** 2" x 1¹/₄".
• Cut 1 strip 1¹/₂" wide. From this strip, cut 5 **horizontal sashings** 1¹/₂" x 5¹/₄".
• Cut 4 **vertical sashings** 1¹/₂" x 34".
• Cut 2 **side inner borders** 1¹/₂" x 34".
• Cut 2 **top/bottom inner borders** 1¹/₂" x 30¹/₄".

From fabric for block bottoms and outer border:
• Cut 4 strips 1¹/₂" wide. From these strips, cut 25 **block bottoms** 5¹/₄" x 1¹/₂".
• Cut 2 **side outer borders** 2¹/₂" x 38".
• Cut 2 **top/bottom outer borders** 2¹/₂" x 36¹/₄".

From fabric for middle border:
• Cut 2 **side middle borders** 1¹/₂" x 36".
• Cut 2 **top/bottom middle borders** 1¹/₂" x 32¹/₄".

From binding fabric:
• Cut 5 **binding strips** 2¹/₄" wide.

Cutting Diagram

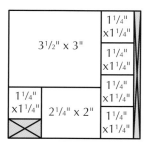

MAKING THE BLOCKS

*Follow **Piecing** and **Pressing**, page 32. Match right sides and use ¹/₄" seam allowances throughout. Measurements given include seam allowances.*

1. For **Block**, select 1 **rectangle A**, 1 **rectangle B**, and 5 **squares** of the same fabric, plus 1 *each* of **rectangles C**, **D**, **E**, and **F**, and 1 **block bottom.**
2. Draw a diagonal line on the wrong side of 3 **squares**.
3. Place 1 **square** on corner of **rectangle C** and stitch along drawn line. Trim ¹/₄" from stitching line **(Fig. 1)** and press open to make **Unit 1**.

Fig. 1   Unit 1

4. In the same manner, use 1 square and **rectangle D** to make **Unit 2**. Use 1 square and **rectangle E** to make **Unit 3**.

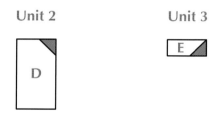

Unit 2   Unit 3

5. Sew **rectangle B** and Unit 3 together, then add Unit 1 to make **Unit 4**. Unit 4 should measure 5¹/₄" x 2³/₄".

Unit 4

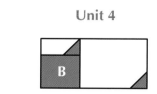

6. Sew 2 squares and **rectangle F** together to make **Unit 5**. Unit 5 should measure 3¹/₂" x 1¹/₄".

Unit 5

7. Sew **rectangle A** and Unit 5 together, then add Unit 2 to make **Unit 6**. Unit 6 should measure 5¹/₄" x 3³/₄".

Unit 6

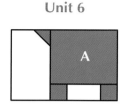

8. Sew Unit 4, Unit 6, and **block bottom** together to make **Block**. Block should measure 5¹/₄" x 7".
9. Repeat Steps 1-8 to make 25 Blocks.

Block (make 25)

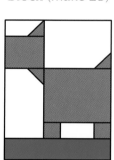

ASSEMBLING THE QUILT TOP

1. Referring to **Quilt Top Diagram** and paying special attention to placement of sashings, sew 1 **horizontal sashing** and 5 Blocks together to make *vertical* **Row**. Row should measure 5¹/₄" x 34". Make 5 Rows.

2. Sew Rows and 4 **vertical sashings** together to make **Quilt Top Center**. Quilt Top Center should measure 28¹/₄" x 34".

3. Matching centers and corners, sew **side** and then **top/bottom inner borders** to **Quilt Top Center**.

4. Matching centers and corners, sew **middle** and **outer borders** to Quilt Top.

COMPLETING THE QUILT

1. Follow **Machine Quilting**, page 33, to mark, layer, and quilt as desired.

2. Follow **Making a Hanging Sleeve**, page 36, to make and attach a hanging sleeve, if desired.

3. Follow **Binding**, page 36, to bind quilt using **binding strips**.

Quilt Top Diagram

NiCOLe

For these versions, you will need ¹/₄ yd (23 cm) of fabric for the block bottoms and ³/₈ yd (34 cm) of fabric for the outer border.

GENERAL INSTRUCTIONS

To make your quilting easier and more enjoyable, we encourage you to carefully read all of the general instructions, study the color photographs, and familiarize yourself with the individual project instructions before beginning a project.

FABRICS

SELECTING FABRICS

Choose high-quality, medium-weight 100% cotton fabrics. All-cotton fabrics hold a crease better, fray less, and are easier to quilt than cotton/polyester blends.

These designs are made using pre-cut charm packs, collections of 5" x 5" squares. Each project lists the number of squares you will need. Always check the number of pieces in a charm pack against your pattern requirements.

Yardage requirements listed for each project are based on 43"/44" wide fabric with a "usable" width of 40" after shrinkage and trimming selvages. Actual usable width will probably vary slightly from fabric to fabric. Our recommended yardage lengths should be adequate for occasional re-squaring of fabric when many cuts are required.

PREPARING FABRICS

We do not recommend pre-washing your yardage or charm squares. Pre-washing fabrics may distort the fabric and may cause the edges to ravel. As a result, your charm squares may not be large enough to cut all of the pieces required for your chosen project.

Prepare fabrics before cutting with a steam iron set on cotton and starch or sizing. The starch or sizing will give the fabric a crisp finish which will make cutting more accurate and may make piecing easier.

ROTARY CUTTING

• Place fabric on work surface with fold closest to you.

• Cut all strips from the selvage-to-selvage width of the fabric.

- Square left edge of fabric using rotary cutter and rulers (**Figs. 1-2**).

Fig. 1

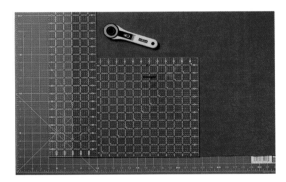

Fig. 2

- To cut each strip required for a project, place ruler over cut edge of fabric, aligning desired marking on ruler with cut edge; make cut (**Fig. 3**).

Fig. 3

- When cutting several strips from a single piece of fabric, it is important to make sure that cuts remain at a perfect right angle to the fold; square fabric as needed.

PIECING

Precise cutting, followed by accurate piecing, will ensure that all pieces of quilt top fit together well.

- Set sewing machine stitch length for approximately 11 stitches per inch.

- Use neutral-colored general-purpose sewing thread (not quilting thread) in needle and in bobbin.

- An accurate $1/4$" seam allowance is **essential**. Presser feet that are $1/4$" wide are available for most sewing machines.

- For an accurate seam allowance when piecing charm squares with pinked edges, measure from point to point across the center of the square. If it measures exactly 5" x 5", align the tip of the points with your $1/4$" seam guide when sewing. It may be necessary to use a "scant" $1/4$" seam allowance. Making a "test block" will determine if any adjustments to your seam allowances are necessary.

- When piecing, always place pieces right sides together and match raw edges; pin if necessary.

- Chain piecing saves time and will usually result in more accurate piecing.

- Trim away points of seam allowances that extend beyond edges of sewn pieces.

SEWING ACROSS SEAM INTERSECTIONS

When sewing across intersection of two seams, place pieces right sides together and match seams exactly, making sure seam allowances are pressed in opposite directions **(Fig. 4)**.

Fig. 4

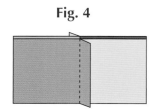

SEWING SHARP POINTS

To ensure sharp points when joining triangular or diagonal pieces, stitch across the center of the "X" (shown in pink) formed on wrong side by previous seams **(Fig. 5)**.

Fig. 5

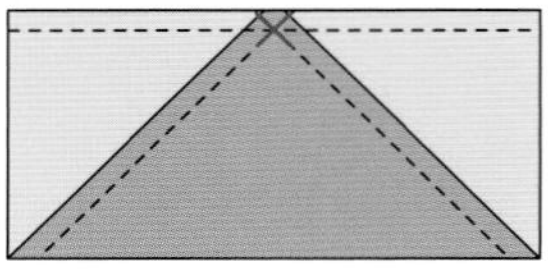

PRESSING

- Use steam iron set on "Cotton" for all pressing.

- Press after sewing each seam.

- Seam allowances are almost always pressed to one side, usually toward darker fabric. However, to reduce bulk it may occasionally be necessary to press seam allowances toward the lighter fabric or even to press them open.

- To prevent a dark fabric seam allowance from showing through light fabric, trim darker seam allowance slightly narrower than lighter seam allowance.

- To press long seams without curving or other distortion, lay strips across width of the ironing board.

- When sewing blocks into rows, seam allowances may be pressed in one direction in odd numbered rows and in the opposite direction in even numbered rows. When sewing rows together, press seam allowances in one direction.

MACHINE QUILTING

*Quilting holds the three layers (top, batting, and backing) of the quilt together. Because marking, layering, and quilting are interrelated and may be done in different orders depending on circumstances, please read entire **Machine Quilting** section, pages 33-35, before beginning project.*

TYPES OF QUILTING DESIGNS

In the Ditch Quilting
Quilting along seamlines or along edges of appliquéd pieces is called "in the ditch" quilting. This type of quilting should be done on side **opposite** the seam allowance and does not have to be marked.

Outline Quilting
Quilting a consistent distance, usually ¹/₄", from seam or appliqué is called "outline" quilting. Outline quilting may be marked, or ¹/₄" masking tape may be placed along seamlines for quilting guide. (Do not leave tape on quilt longer than necessary, since it may leave an adhesive residue.)

Motif Quilting
Quilting a design, such as a feathered wreath, is called "motif" quilting. This type of quilting should be marked before basting quilt layers together.

Echo Quilting
Quilting that follows the outline of an appliquéd or pieced design with two or more parallel lines is called "echo" quilting. This type of quilting does not need to be marked.

Meandering Quilting
Quilting in random curved lines and swirls is called "meandering" quilting. Quilting lines should not cross or touch each other. This type of quilting does not need to be marked.

MARKING QUILTING LINES
Quilting lines may be marked using fabric marking pencils, chalk markers, or water- or air-soluble pens.

Simple quilting designs may be marked with chalk or chalk pencil after basting. A small area may be marked, then quilted, before moving to next area to be marked. Intricate designs should be marked before basting using a more durable marker.

Caution: Pressing may permanently set some marks. **Test** different markers **on scrap fabric** to find one that marks clearly and can be thoroughly removed.

A wide variety of pre-cut quilting stencils, as well as entire books of quilting patterns, are available. Using a stencil makes it easier to mark intricate or repetitive designs.

To make a stencil from a pattern, center template plastic over pattern and use a permanent marker to trace pattern onto plastic. Use a craft knife with single or double blade to cut channels along traced lines (**Fig. 6**).

Fig. 6

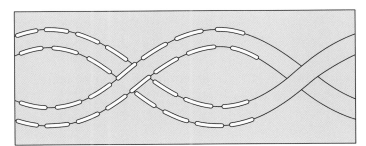

PREPARING THE BACKING

To allow for slight shifting of quilt top during quilting, backing should be approximately 4" larger on all sides. Yardage requirements listed for quilt backings are calculated for 43"/44" wide fabric. To piece a backing using 43"/44" wide fabric, use the following instructions.

1. Measure length and width of quilt top; add 8" to each measurement.
2. Cut backing fabric into two lengths the determined **length** measurement. Trim selvages. Place lengths with right sides facing and sew long edges together, forming a tube (**Fig. 7**). Match seams and press along one fold (**Fig. 8**). Cut along pressed fold to form single piece (**Fig. 9**).

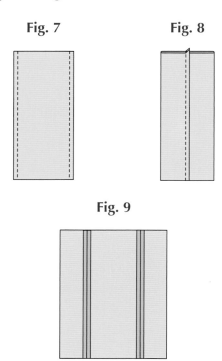

Fig. 7   Fig. 8

Fig. 9

3. Trim backing to size determined in Step 1; press seam allowances open.

CHOOSING THE BATTING

The appropriate batting will make quilting easier. For fine hand quilting, choose low-loft batting. All cotton or cotton/polyester blend battings work well for machine quilting because the cotton helps "grip" quilt layers. If quilt is to be tied, a high-loft batting, sometimes called extra-loft or fat batting, may be used to make quilt "fluffy."

Types of batting include cotton, polyester, wool, cotton/polyester blend, cotton/wool blend, and silk.

When selecting batting, refer to package labels for characteristics and care instructions. Cut batting same size as prepared backing.

ASSEMBLING THE QUILT

1. Examine wrong side of quilt top closely; trim any seam allowances and clip any threads that may show through front of the quilt. Press quilt top, being careful not to "set" any marked quilting lines.
2. Place backing **wrong** side up on flat surface. Use masking tape to tape edges of backing to surface. Place batting on top of backing fabric. Smooth batting gently, being careful not to stretch or tear. Center quilt top **right** side up on batting.
3. Use 1" rustproof safety pins to "pin-baste" all layers together, spacing pins approximately 4" apart. Begin at center and work toward outer edges to secure all layers. If possible, place pins away from areas that will be quilted, although pins may be removed as needed when quilting.

MACHINE QUILTING METHODS

Use general-purpose thread in bobbin. Do not use quilting thread. Thread the needle of machine with general-purpose thread or transparent monofilament thread to make quilting blend with quilt top fabrics. Use decorative thread, such as a metallic or contrasting-color general-purpose thread, to make quilting lines stand out more.

Straight-Line Quilting

The term "straight-line" is somewhat deceptive, since curves (especially gentle ones) as well as straight lines can be stitched with this technique.

1. Set stitch length for six to ten stitches per inch and attach walking foot to sewing machine.
2. Determine which section of quilt will have longest continuous quilting line, oftentimes area from center top to center bottom. Roll up and secure each edge of quilt to help reduce the bulk, keeping fabrics smooth. Smaller projects may not need to be rolled.
3. Begin stitching on longest quilting line, using very short stitches for the first 1/4" to "lock" quilting. Stitch across project, using one hand on each side of walking foot to slightly spread fabric and to guide fabric through machine. Lock stitches at end of quilting line.
4. Continue machine quilting, stitching longer quilting lines first to stabilize quilt before moving on to other areas.

Free-Motion Quilting

Free-motion quilting may be free form or may follow a marked pattern.

1. Attach darning foot to sewing machine and lower or cover feed dogs.
2. Position quilt under darning foot; lower foot. Holding top thread, take a stitch and pull bobbin thread to top of quilt. To "lock" beginning of quilting line, hold top and bobbin threads while making three to five stitches in place.
3. Use one hand on each side of darning foot to slightly spread fabric and to move fabric through the machine. Even stitch length is achieved by using smooth, flowing hand motion and steady machine speed. Slow machine speed and fast hand movement will create long stitches. Fast machine speed and slow hand movement will create short stitches. Move quilt sideways, back and forth, in a circular motion, or in a random motion to create desired designs; do not rotate quilt. Lock stitches at end of each quilting line.

MAKING A HANGING SLEEVE

Attaching a hanging sleeve to the back of a quilt before the binding is added allows the project to be displayed on a wall.

1. Measure width of quilt top edge and subtract 1". Cut piece of fabric 7" wide by determined measurement.
2. Press short edges of fabric piece ¼" to wrong side; press edges ¼" to wrong side again and machine stitch in place.
3. Matching wrong sides, fold piece in half lengthwise to form a tube.
4. Follow project instructions to sew binding to quilt top and to trim backing and batting. Before Blindstitching binding to backing, match raw edges and stitch hanging sleeve to center top edge on back of quilt.
5. Finish binding quilt, treating hanging sleeve as part of backing.
6. Blindstitch bottom of hanging sleeve to backing, taking care not to stitch through to front of quilt.
7. Insert dowel or slat into hanging sleeve.

BINDING

Binding encloses the raw edges of quilt.

1. Using a diagonal seam (**Fig. 10**), sew binding strips called for in project together end to end.

Fig. 10

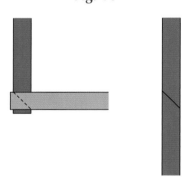

2. Matching wrong sides and long edges, press strip in half to make binding.
3. Beginning with one end near center on bottom edge of quilt, lay binding around quilt to make sure that seams in binding will not end up at a corner. Adjust placement if necessary. Matching raw edges of binding to raw edge of quilt top, pin binding to right side of quilt along one edge.
4. When you reach first corner, mark ¼" from corner of quilt top (**Fig. 11**).

Fig. 11

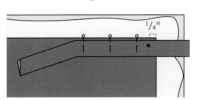

5. Beginning approximately 10" from end of binding and using ¼" seam allowance, sew binding to quilt, backstitching at beginning of stitching and at mark (**Fig. 12**). Lift needle out of fabric and clip thread.

Fig. 12

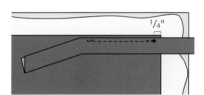

6. Fold binding as shown in **Figs. 13-14** and pin binding to adjacent side, matching raw edges. When you've reached the next corner, mark ¼" from edge of quilt top.

Fig. 13   **Fig. 14**

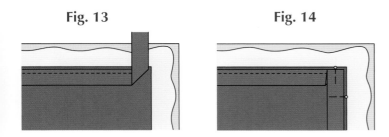

7. Backstitching at edge of quilt top, sew pinned binding to quilt (**Fig. 15**); backstitch at the next mark. Lift needle out of fabric and clip thread.

Fig. 15

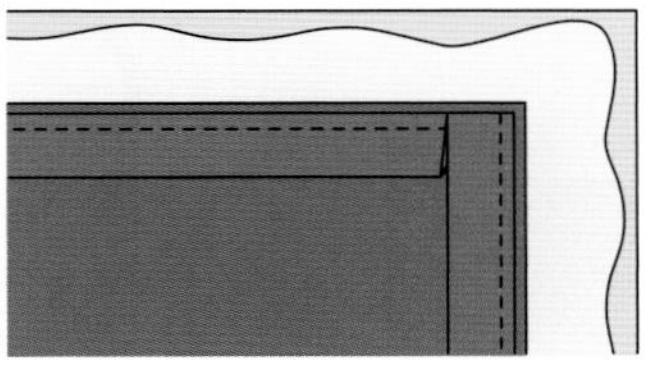

8. Continue sewing binding to quilt, stopping approximately 10" from starting point (**Fig. 16**).

Fig. 16

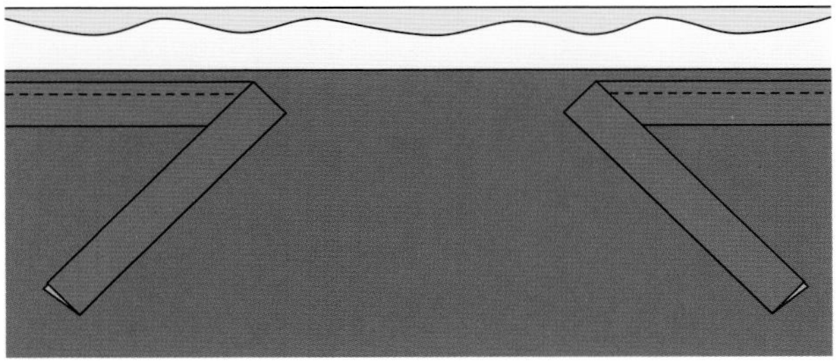

9. Bring beginning and end of binding to center of opening and fold each end back, leaving a ¼" space between folds (**Fig. 17**). Finger press folds.

Fig. 17

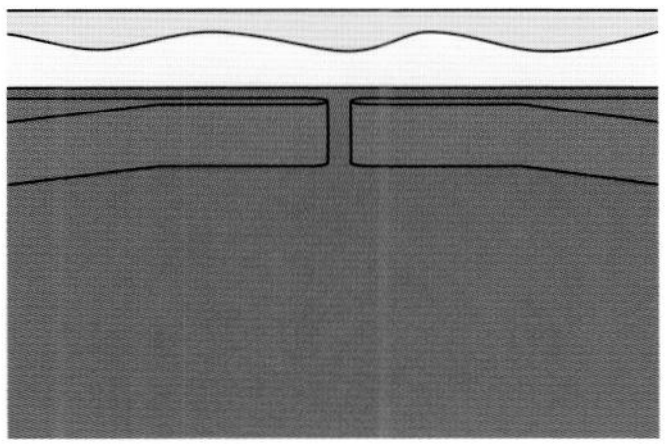

10. Unfold ends of binding and draw a line across wrong side in finger-pressed crease. Draw a line through the lengthwise pressed fold of binding at the same spot to create a cross mark. With edge of ruler at cross mark, line up 45° angle marking on ruler with one long side of binding. Draw a diagonal line from edge to edge. Repeat on remaining end, making sure that the two diagonal lines are angled the same way (**Fig. 18**).

Fig. 18

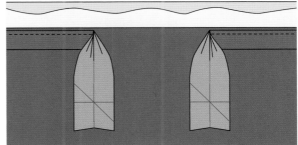

11. Matching right sides and diagonal lines, pin binding ends together at right angles **(Fig. 19)**.

Fig. 19

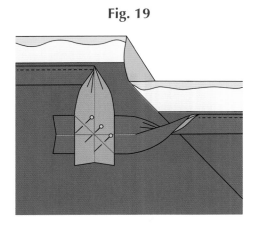

12. Machine stitch along diagonal line **(Fig. 20)**, removing pins as you stitch.

Fig. 20

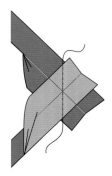

13. Lay binding against quilt to double check that it is correct length.

14. Trim binding ends, leaving ¹/₄" seam allowance; press seam open. Stitch binding to quilt.

15. Trim backing and batting even with edges of quilt top.

16. On one edge of quilt, fold binding over to quilt backing and pin pressed edge in place, covering stitching line **(Fig. 21)**. On adjacent side, fold binding over, forming a mitered corner **(Fig. 22)**. Repeat to pin remainder of binding in place.

Fig. 21   **Fig. 22**

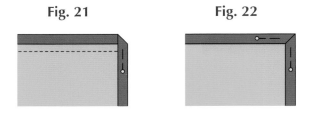

17. Blindstitch binding to backing, taking care not to stitch through to front of quilt. To Blindstitch, come up at 1, go down at 2, and come up at 3 **(Fig. 23)**.

Fig. 23

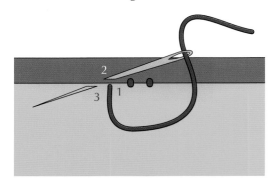

fabrics used

As we all know, fabrics that are available in stores today may not be available six months from now. Sometimes when fabrics are no longer available in stores, they may be available on the Internet. For your convenience, we have listed the fabrics used for our quilts below.

HANNAH
- Reunion by Sweetwater for Moda
- Vintage Modern by Bonnie and Camille for Moda
- Tend The Earth by Deb Strain for Moda

INGRID
- Terrain by Kate Spain for Moda
- Pezzy Print by Sandy Klop for Moda
- Salt Air by Cosmo Cricket for Moda

JENNIFER
- Ten Little Things by Jenn Ski for Moda
- Cape Ann by Oliver + S for Moda
- Hello Luscious by BasicGrey for Moda

KENDRA
- Dilly Dally by Me and My Sister Designs for Moda
- Petite Odile by French General for Moda
- Custom Charm Pack using Hoffman Key Lime Batiks

LESLIE
- Good Morning by Me and My Sister Designs for Moda
- Farmers Market by Brannock and Patek for Moda
- California Girl by Fig Tree and Co. for Moda

MOLLY
- Twirl by Me and My Sister Designs for Moda
- Puttin' on the Ritz by Bunny Hill Designs for Moda
- Curio by BasicGrey for Moda

NICOLE
- A Stitch in Color by Malka Dubrawsky for Moda
- Custom black and white Charm Pack from individual quilt store/Borders are Twirl and Dilly Dally by Me and My Sister Designs for Moda
- Joy by Kate Spain for Moda

Metric Conversion Chart	
Inches x 2.54 = centimeters (cm)	Yards x .9144 = meters (m)
Inches x 25.4 = millimeters (mm)	Yards x 91.44 = centimeters (cm)
Inches x .0254 = meters (m)	Centimeters x .3937 = inches (")
	Meters x 1.0936 = yards (yd)

Standard Equivalents

1/8"	3.2 mm	0.32 cm	1/8 yard	11.43 cm	0.11 m
1/4"	6.35 mm	0.635 cm	1/4 yard	22.86 cm	0.23 m
3/8"	9.5 mm	0.95 cm	3/8 yard	34.29 cm	0.34 m
1/2"	12.7 mm	1.27 cm	1/2 yard	45.72 cm	0.46 m
5/8"	15.9 mm	1.59 cm	5/8 yard	57.15 cm	0.57 m
3/4"	19.1 mm	1.91 cm	3/4 yard	68.58 cm	0.69 m
7/8"	22.2 mm	2.22 cm	7/8 yard	80 cm	0.8 m
1"	25.4 mm	2.54 cm	1 yard	91.44 cm	0.91 m

FOR Barbara groves & mary jacobson,

getting started in the quilt design business began with their very first quilting class. The quilt shop hosting their beginner's class was for sale, which made the sisters think how much fun it would be to have their own shop. Years later, they did indeed open a quilt shop. Designing and sewing samples for the store was one of their favorite things to do. Eventually, they sold the store to give their full attention to designing quilts—and that was the beginning of Me & My Sister Designs. They've been quilting together for seventeen creative years, and this is their fifth pattern book available through www.leisurearts.com. To see the sweet and whimsical fabrics that Barb and Mary have designed for Moda, visit meandmysisterdesigns.com.

Quilts shown were quilted by Sharon Elsberry.

Production Team: Technical Editor – Lisa Lancaster; Technical Writer – Frances Huddleston; Graphic Artist – Becca Snider Tally, Kara Darling and Jessica Bramlett; Photo Stylist – Sondra Daniel; Photographer – Ken West.

We have made every effort to ensure that these instructions are accurate and complete. We cannot, however, be responsible for human error, typographical mistakes, or variations in individual work.